NO LONGER ARRESTED!

NO LONGER ARRESTED!

Kellee Williams

Kellee Williams

Published by CLF Publishing, LLC. 3281 Guasti Road, Seventh Floor, Ontario, CA 91761. (760) 669-8149.

Copyright © 2012 by Kellee Williams. All rights reserved. No portion of this book may be reproduced, stored in a retrieval system, or transmitted by any form or any means electronically, photocopied, recorded, or any other except for brief quotations in printed reviews, without the prior permission of the publisher.

Cover Design by Senir Design. Contact information- info@senirdesign.com.

ISBN # 978-0-9884237-6-3

Printed in the United States of America.

Dedications

To my three beautiful children: Kaalan Scott, Kaasey Stoan, Kalaon Shaunelle and my precious grandson, Kane Lyon.
Just to let you guys know that mommy is "No Longer Arrested." Physically, mentally, emotionally, and especially spiritually! I am free, and I bless the name of the Most High God for all three of you. You have stood by your mother through some of the toughest times, and I am grateful!

I thank the Most High God for all of you, and I'm blessed to have the best, strongest and loving children in the world! I love you! I could not have done this without you and your love and forgiveness! I pray the blessings of God all over you!

Acknowledgements

Before I thank anyone, I do so graciously give honor to God, my father, Jesus Christ, His precious son, the Holy Ghost, for He is my comforter!

There are no words to express or convey how much I love and appreciate my mother, Willie Williams-Allen. She was woven with a special thread by God. She may have wanted to give up, but she didn't. She may have wanted to fall apart, but that "thread" held her together! That same thread held our family; thank you Jesus Christ!

Many people have been a part of my life, had an impact on my life for a reason, season or a lifetime. I want to thank all of you because in some way or another, you helped pave the way for this book and my success!

I acknowledge every man who beat me, every person who talked about me, laughed at me, and the ones who raped me. Not only of my physical body, but my self-esteem as well! My family and friends who thought I was garbage for having a disease of addiction, a sickness of weakness. The family member who molested, raped and tortured me, may he rest in peace! I make this acknowledgement not to make you feel bad or guilty but to say, I forgive you! I publicly and wholeheartedly say "May God bless you!"

Now, to my pastors, Charles and Rosalind Travis! You are truly sent by God to be my shepherds, my covering, my mentors, my advisors, counselors, and my spiritual parents. You have no idea how much I love you for standing with me, praying for me, pulling and loving me through it all!

I love you all. God bless!!

No Longer Arrested!

CHAPTER ONE

"I should give you seven years," said the judge, with such a stern, serious look on his face. "However, since you are the only one in the court room, and there's no one to hear me give you favor, I will sentence you to sixteen months in the state penitentiary."

One single tear fell from my eye as I looked at him and knew in my heart that it was not him giving me favor, but it was Jesus Christ making intercession for me to the Father. As I was being read the stipulations of my sentence and where I would spend the next nine months and twenty days of my life, I began to rejoice in my spirit because I was truly grateful not to have received those seven years!

In the holding cell with the women who came on the ride with me from Central Detention Center (CDC) in San Bernardino to the Fontana Superior Court Building, some were going home, one was sentenced to seven years (ironic huh?), and some were on probation, I not one time questioned God. I wanted Him to comfort them more than me.

While in CDC awaiting my fate, God allowed me to start prayer circles and encourage the women around me. We would sing praises unto God and cry; I saw God move in that place and in me. I saw Him heal deliver and set free right there in our cells. One lady I met came in with a faith that I had not seen before. She praised the Lord and prayed boldly before us and the throne. She encouraged my praise! She confessed her innocence so adamantly and with a shout of victory. When she came back from court that next day, she shouted and cried, "I knew the Lord wouldn't let me down!"

I knew at that point I would trust God like never before! He had boosted my faith and fanned my flame. I was ready to go!

This was my first time going to a state penitentiary. I was very nervous, but not afraid. I was expecting God to bring me through and not just get me through, but change my life! I had heard stories of how the state penitentiary was so much better than the county prisons. You were able to wear your own clothes, eat real food (the stuff they fed us in the county was awful), have boxes sent in (with the items from a list they would provide), and have visits. The best perk of all for me was going to church with a choir and ministers who would come in from the outside and share the love and hope of Christ with us. I had heard the stories of the "lifers" and women who looked just like men. I just had to, I guess, see it for myself!

Words cannot explain the feeling of loneliness that had tried to take over as I rode the prison bus six hours to Chowchilla State Prison for Women. "No talking," the police officers yelled. "Face forward and if you need to talk then you talk to us." I thought, "How do you ride six hours somewhere without talking?" I also thought I was rid of those disgusting sack lunches with green meat inside, rotten fruit and nothing to wash down the hard stale bread; that was our lunch when we pulled into a gas station and into an empty lot next door to eat. It was hard to eat while chained at your waist and your hands also chained. The officers were watching with hawk eyes as the shotguns stood tall in the front of the bus. Even the hard core girls were silenced during this ride to the State Penn. I guess nobody is as really hard core as one would think.

All the stories and descriptions failed in comparison to the real thing. As the bus drove through the high, barbed-wire gates, there was a tower with a man strapped with a shotgun as we entered the grounds. My heart raced, and I thought, "Lord, what have I done?" I began to pray and ask God for help beyond measure, to be a fence all around me.

Once we were issued our state clothing, we were cavity searched, interviewed by a counselor and seen by a doctor. Then, we were escorted to "reception" ("A" Yard, supposedly known as Camp Snoopy. There are four yards- each with a letter). I looked at all the concrete and iron and thought who would leave here and actually come back. (I'll get to that part later). There were police everywhere with bullet proof vests, sticks, mace and tazers.

When I got to my cell, the first thing I asked for was a Bible. The girl in there with me informed me that they were scarce, but I could put in a request for one. "Ok, when do I get to go to church?" I asked. I knew then, I needed to get my foundation under me to withstand the encounter of being 'ARRESTED'! Sure, I've had other encounters with the law and city jails, but nothing like this!!

I was closed in a two-man cell for hours and hours at a time. I only got a chance to shower every other day. I had to run to the shower to be able to take one before the water grew cold. I had to wear a Mumu (moomoo) for two to three weeks until I could move into a dorm; all these things seemed so dismal and bleak, but all I could hold on to was the thought that this wasn't going to last always!

Those hours I spent in that cell, I would read my bible, and thankfully my 'cellie' was a believer. That also made it easier to bear. She was a tiny, white girl with a lot of spunk, who seemed to be out of place just like me.

We shared stories, hopes, dreams and laughter. We both vowed to do all we could never to see that place again. If our day to shower fell on a Sunday, we would be so excited because we could go to church. Well, that is, church would come to us. We weren't allowed at the chapel with general population (Yards B-D) until classified. The women of Aglow Ministries would come in and sing with such joy and hope. They would tell us of the love Jesus Christ has for us and that we have not been forgotten!

Now, I have been in church all my life, in the choir, on the usher board, and in contests where I would write and speak about Christ. I even went to a prison at age fifteen to sing, and it was then that something was birthed in me to be a part of a prison ministry as I became older. Never did I think or even imagine I'd have to go into the prisons as an inmate to do so. I know now that that was the best way to go to reach God's people!

Even going to church as an adult and in my active drug use, I'd go out on Saturday night and make it home by 6am Sunday morning, in time to take a shower and get to the church house. I was sick, and I needed a hospital (church) and a physician (Jesus Christ). So, I would think I knew about God and how He moved because of religion. I did not realize a relationship was needed. A relationship is a divine connection between me, my soul and Jesus Christ. As I was taught this and had an open and willing spirit to get this connection, I knew I was changing.

One Sunday after being classified and making it "over the wall" from reception to where my time would be spent on "D" yard, I went to church in the chapel. How excited I was!

On the way from my dorm to the chapel, I saw women and men dressed and I actually thought one woman was a man. I said, "Oh, how fine he is." The girls I was walking with laughed at me...that was a woman! I couldn't tell. I came across some dressed in their gang garb and ones playing sports. There were blankets everywhere with radios and oldies playing as if at the park around the corner from my house or something. Some had food they made in the dorms and brought out to share. I witnessed a wedding between two women and even saw a couple making out on a blanket. What shocked me most was the use of drugs and drinking right on the yard on my way to the chapel.

The line to get in the chapel was outside along the wall. The chapel was small. I thought it was going to a big building because there were so many women - surely there had to be a big church. Much to my chagrin, there wasn't. However, the spirit of the Lord God was "BIG". The anointing was heavy and the ministry team that was there blessed my soul. That was the boost I needed!

I didn't look back! I joined the choir and was able to read a few of my poems to encourage the ladies at different services. God told me to start a prayer circle in the card room (where they played cards, dominoes, played music, etc.) at seven every morning. I did. When they saw me coming in the mornings, they began to give way to the Holy Ghost. The circle grew so big; we had to move out into the dorm area. Bless the Lord in all His Splendor and Glory!!

My relationship with Jesus Christ began to grow in leaps and bounds. No matter what I was faced with, I knew if I just held on to His unchanging hand, I'd be alright. I'd be better than alright. I'd be free, no more shackles, handcuffs, bondage or weight. I'd be no longer arrested! I may be within the confines of prison walls, but my spirit, the Spirit of the risen Savior; Jesus Christ was within me!

I was taken to a higher height in my praise and worship. My prayer life was keen to what was going on around me. At any given moment, I was praying with someone, for someone or just walking with Jesus Christ praying and tearing down strongholds around the yard. I was excited about what was happening to me!

Time has gone by, and it was close to me going home. I had heard rumors to not to discuss your release date because someone who had more time than you (ten years to life) could easily turn your nine months and twenty days to three years. So, I was nervous and began to walk on eggshells just wanting to go home safely. At one service, a minister told me that what God has for me is for me and nobody could take that from me. I relaxed and kept my mind stayed on Jesus Christ!

The week before I was to be released, an evangelist from the outside, who had come in to do the Lord's work, asked my name. I told her Treasure because that was the name I used. She got excited and grabbed her bible and turned to Isaiah 45:2-3. She proceeded to tell me that I am a Treasure true enough in God's eyes. That He would go ahead of me and break the gates of brass and these iron bars, just for me. So there was no doubting that I would be released and on time with no incident. That became one of my favorite scriptures. I use it now for my prison ministry.

CHAPTER TWO

Released on March 14, 2001, the wait of actually being released and free was taxing on my patience. They wanted to search us again, fingerprint us again, and have us wait again. When my name was called, I signed a paper to have my things sent home ahead of me and one for my "gate money," the $200.00 dollars they gave us to get home on, eat, etc. Some bought their beer, cigarettes and weed right at the station. I was so glad to be able to go to the restroom, buy food and call my mother. Nothing else mattered to me. I knew that drugs were the reason I was arrested in the first place. I had not one thought of buying dope. I knew I had to see my parole officer that next morning and was scared of the unknown.

As I rode home, I prayed and asked God to shield me from the devil. I couldn't do this on my own. I remember quoting Psalm 23. Over and over I said, "He prepares a table before me in the presence of mine enemies" (vs. 5). All I wanted to do was sit at this table and be safe with Jesus Christ!

My sister picked me up from the bus station and took me home. My boys were waiting outside for me, and I was so glad to see them. They ran to me and I to them. Thank you, Jesus Christ for another chance!!

My mother hugged me and told me she was happy I made it safely. It was good to be home. I showered, ate, watched television, and went to sleep, with anticipation of my parole visit.

No Longer Arrested!

There was a knock at the door; it was Ms. Holland, my parole officer. She had short brown hair, and she was tall and thin. I could see the vest and gun under her shirt. I introduced myself and my mother, and I began telling her how glad I was to be home. Immediately with no forethought, she cut me off and said, "I don't want to hear that church stuff. Everybody gets out and goes to church and does well for the first few weeks; but, keep it up," she continued, "I'll see." As she searched my room, my closet for weapons, drugs etc. she seemed disappointed almost that there weren't any. Afterwards, she gave me her card and what she expected of me and left. I was relieved. It wasn't as bad as I thought it would be. I'll be glad when it's over though!

I started looking for work immediately. I went to the unemployment office and also filled out applications around the Rialto area, where I lived at the time. So far so good; I had no temptations, no urges, or dreams. I was going to church and being active.

God blessed me with a job and I worked, went to church, and spent time with my children. It was time for my parole officer to come and visit again. I was actually anticipating her visit because I was clean and doing what was required of me. The visit came, but it wasn't her. It was a man. He was very nice, and I even offered him a cup of coffee. We got along well, and he told me he wouldn't worry about me. I would go into the office once a month to drug test, and he would come and visit. Well, he only came out once and all my tests were clean. I was released from parole on time (thirteen months) without a hitch. Glory to God!! I was proud of myself for a change!

CHAPTER THREE

I became involved in several ministries at my church (LPH), and I even drove the church van at one time. Believing I was well on my way, I was asked to speak at church, was a member of leadership, and on the board. God even blessed me with an awesome man who loved Jesus Christ more than I, and I thought *This is it!* If someone had told me I would mess that up, I would have called him/her a liar. Low and behold, I did! I relapsed! I messed up everything. It came so subtly and quick. I didn't even see it coming-remember, no dreams, no temptation, and no urges. I was off parole and doing well. So I thought!

I became a functioning addict. I worked and was still going to church. I would get off work and catch a cab to the dope house and come home in time to go to work the next day. I would be exhausted, and my head pounded from the strong and long drinking. Daytime seemed to be my enemy. I wished it was nighttime all the time.

At work one day, I remembered I was quite an intelligent person with numbers and that recollection led me to do some not so intelligent things and make some not so intelligent decisions. One was to embezzle money from the workplace. I began to take a little money here, a little there, in increments of $60 dollars, so as not to get noticed. Again, I thought I had become "good" at it, and I was the dealer's best customer! He was glad to see me coming. I even had a hook up for him in the electronics department. One day, I went to work, and it was on my day off (being greedy). I counted down my drawer and proceeded to clock out. I had already gone to the bathroom (one of my trips) to put money away. As I was going to my locker, my manager called me to her office; my heart dropped, I knew I was busted!

In her office was a short clean cut caucasian man with glasses. He smelled good and had a pleasant look on his face. That didn't matter at all; it didn't erase the thought of me going to prison for the second time. I was escorted and taken into the care of West Valley Detention Center.

Arrested again! Going through the very thing I was wondering how others did this during my first go 'round. There I was in this humiliating circumstance yet again. Bend over, cough, sit, stand, no over there, over here, all over again. The smell, the sound of hollowness, the very darkness that I would surround myself with was not an option …it was a reality! It had encompassed me in this place. How I'd like to see the daylight which I thought was my enemy. Isaiah 52 (paraphrased) says God is asking the captive- daughters of Zion, "What is this? Why are my people enslaved again and oppressed without excuse? I brought you out, and you return to be enslaved yet again?"

The darkness was all around me. I tried to pray. I tried to smile. I couldn't even talk. I wanted to remain the woman of God I was called to be. I wanted to encourage someone else, so I could feel better, but I just couldn't. The memories of my past flooded my mind. "Look at you. You'll never be anything." I knew it was the enemy but it was my voice inside me I heard so plainly.

Growing up in a loving Christian home, I was always involved in my church as a youth. I was active in sports at school and scored high academically. I graduated on the honor roll and passed my entrance exams to attend the University of Arkansas at Little Rock, where I would major in Journalism. I was well on my way. The fact that I had already been introduced to cocaine before I went away to school didn't interfere with my going away to school.

I met my oldest son's father in college, and I was planning to be married, but it didn't work out; so at four and a half months pregnant, I flew back to California, and I stayed until Kaalan was born.

Shortly afterward, my total dysfunction began. I met someone who said he loved me, and I fell for it. It didn't take long before the abuse started and the indulging of cocaine as well. Being married to a drug dealer made my drug abuse easy. It didn't seem as though I was addicted because I was still functioning, and I hadn't sold any of my possessions nor my body. I knew something was wrong when I would send my son to my mother to keep him free from the arguing, the fighting, the drug use, and the drinking. However, I continued, and it seemed this was the only thing to help the hurt, pain, and low self-esteem that I was sinking into deeper and deeper.

I didn't care about living on the hill in Altadena, CA and had everything I wanted. I wasn't happy! I was sick! The sickening part about it was I didn't realize I was sick.

I stopped going to church even though I'd pray, but my prayers, I thought, would go unanswered. God heard me, but I didn't hear Him. How alone I was. How miserable and defeated I had become. Who was this person? Where did she come from?

After an incident where my ex-husband shot at me and my friend was shot instead, the police were called and blood was everywhere; I was arrested and taken to the Pasadena Police Station; I vowed never to get high again.

No Longer Arrested!

CHAPTER FOUR

No Longer Arrested!

My first rehab experience was at St. Luke Hospital, Pasadena, Calif. I didn't think it was for me, even though I began to attend the meetings and sometimes participate. The meds they gave me in there were more than I was taking on the streets. I thought they were trying to cause me not to function, instead of teaching me how to do so.

Therefore, one night while it was pouring down rain, I packed my bag. I went down the stairs instead of the elevator of the hospital, and I left. I called my husband (ex), and he almost didn't come for me. So, I began walking, and there he was. I had to hear about how I was a failure of course, but I wasn't in that place for me, it was for him, and needless to say, it didn't work!

My insanity started all over again. While awaiting the court's decision on what would be his fate for attempted murder and assault on me, I was high. I didn't like going to court, and I couldn't wait to get home to indulge. I needed the drugs to medicate, to cover up, to drown the anguish, the loneliness and guilt I was having trouble dealing with.

One last court date, they offered him a deal. If he went to trial and lost, he'd get fifteen to life, but because he was a veteran and had his own business, with no priors (not even a traffic citation) he was offered four years with half. He took the deal and I thought I was free. He was the one arrested instead of me. However, my bondage and torment had just begun!

I moved back home with my mother and son. I got involved in trafficking, selling and smoking really tough. Another abusive man came along, and we together were ruthless. We were both Crips (gang members), and that made life even more interesting, if you will. He didn't hit me as much because he spent a lot of time with other women. Nevertheless, I was an accident waiting to happen.

Meanwhile, as I thought about my past and all I had been through, I was still sitting on that cold slab of concrete waiting to be booked, fingerprinted, and given another ugly orange jumpsuit. Two pair of cheap panties that unraveled with the first wash, one pair of socks, to wash out daily, and one bra that I would just have to hope would fit. The hygiene bag (a Ziploc) contained: a generic bar of soap, nasty toothpaste and a toothbrush- the size for a doll, a small, black hair comb which the teeth easily bent and a washcloth.

I tried my best not to look at this as the end, but the beginning. If I could just get out of this! I'd be ok! My past flooded my present and seemingly dim future. I was convinced that I was meant for darkness, gloom and being arrested. Not only in my physical body, but my spiritual and mental just the same. I really was tired though, and I did ask God to help me. I did ask Him: Why am I like this? Why couldn't I get clean and stay clean? Was I going to die like this? And would I make it to heaven?

According to the life I was living-the answer was a resounding "NO!" You will not make it to heaven! It was obvious! I wanted to change, I wanted to stop, I wanted to live, and I wanted to go to heaven. At that moment, I didn't have a clue of what to do because everything I had done up to that point had failed. Something had to give; something had to change! I had to surrender my will and my life over to God! It was easier said than done!

Finally, they called my name, and I went through the booking process which seemed to take forever. It was cold. Some women were complaining and some were sharing their war stories and some were trying desperately to get a call through to anyone who would accept. Me? This was my second rodeo, so I just rode it out. I surely didn't want to be there. I knew I had done wrong though, and I had gotten caught, so I had to pay the piper.

I asked for a speedy removal from the county facility, so I'd get my sentence started. I had been blessed with sixteen months again when they wanted to give me four years. Now I knew I had to change. I had to stop because this way of life wasn't the answer. I didn't want to be a part of the revolving door system.

My stay in West Valley Detention Center was two weeks, and while there, I participated in bible studies, went to the services on Sunday, even though we watched via television. The preacher would come to the jailhouse, but only on the men's side, and we got the monitor. Whatever it took for me to get it, I wanted it. I wanted and I needed to hear the Word of God! I needed to know that there was yet hope for me still.

I would pray with the ladies and we'd exchange stories with one another of how tired we were and prayerfully we'd change. We'd stop this time! Also, we thanked God for another chance to get it right and He didn't allow the enemy to devour us in our mess. How grateful we were!

Well, Tuesday morning at five in the morning, they came to take me and the others to Chowchilla. There came the chains. I could hear the police dragging them as they walked down the corridor to where we were waiting in the holding cells. This was the worst part, being chained like some animal and to another person. Nevertheless, it wasn't enough to keep me from winding up there for the second time though.

The bus ride was long, and we had to be silent all the way. I prayed most of the way and asked God to do something different in me, so I would not find myself repeating this life style. I asked Him for help and strength and I asked Him not to leave me at Chowchilla this time!

CHAPTER FIVE

I became a clerk in the reception dorm on "A" yard. I was able to stay out of the eight-man (woman) room most of the day, and that made it easier to cope. I enjoyed being the clerk. I ran errands, I helped with canteen each week, but most of all, I was allowed to go to both church services on Sundays. I would read poems and attempt to sing sometimes. There was something different going on inside me. No matter what came my way, I tried to be as happy and as positive as I could. I would encourage the ladies around me, and I even paid my tithes by helping them with hygiene and treats (10% of my money each month). I continued to do this until my release.

As time went by, I started to wonder why I was on "A" yard so long. I was told it was very crowded, and it would take longer than usual to see my counselor, so I would be moved. After eight weeks, I saw my counselor, and I was transferred to Live Oak in Yuba City where there was only two hundred women in the facility. This was known as minimum security.

I was able to pack all my pictures, letters, stationary, canteen, hygiene, etc. I took my things and myself over the wall (again) and waited some more to be transferred to Live Oak. I heard it was in a residential neighborhood, and the food was really good. They weren't quite as lenient as the staff in Chowchilla because of the minimum security. They didn't put up with a lot of nonsense or we'd be shipped back to the big house. I didn't care, anywhere but Chowchilla State Prison for Women.

The ladies that were to be transferred with me, we had struck up a special comradeship. We ate together, went to church together and were housed in the same dorm while we waited to be boarded.

It was a beautiful, sunny day in February when we left. The ride was really long, but we managed to have a conversation or two without being yelled at. We laughed softly and talked about new beginnings and hope in Jesus Christ. I was really impressed with one of the lady's belief and enthusiasm level. We became fast friends. Her name is Eileen Orange, and we are still friends this day. What an awesome woman of God. A lot of people misunderstood her, but God allowed me to be open-minded and open-hearted where she was concerned. I got to Live Oak first, and the next week, we were reunited. God immediately began to work in us and through us. We both knew this had to be it!

I joined the choir where another lady would bless my life. Her name is Lucretia Johnson (Trish). She was the choir director and my best friend and confidant still today. We saw the hardships of the young women there, and we prayed with them and encouraged them. Some needed letters to CPS, attorneys, families, etc. Due to bad choices and decisions, they lost their children. I know how that felt because I didn't have my daughter.

We saw God move mightily in those ladies' lives. They began to come to church and give their lives to Christ. Some Sundays, there'd be standing room only. There were outside churches that would come in and bless our socks off! The hunger and thirst after righteousness was being filled.

One of the churches, Mt. Olivet Baptist Church, Carl Dorn, Pastor, would come in on Saturdays for bible study, and we had a high time in the Lord. Trish, Orange, and I learned so much from them and Pastor Dorn allowed us to facilitate programs. Once a month, we'd give different ones assignments and the church would be full. We would sing Zion songs unto the Lord, and He would bless us in return. Ladies were being filled with the Holy Ghost and getting baptized by water and by the Spirit. Sometimes, the guards would have to come and tell us it was time to go in for count. We would just keep going until they'd tell us to stop. I didn't know I'd have this much fun in prison.

I asked God to free me and strengthen me and give me peace, and He did! Right in that place, right in the middle of the neighborhood! Where God blessed me to see children going to the ice cream truck and fireworks on the 4th of July! John 8:36 says, "Therefore, if the Son makes you free, you shall be free indeed!"

No Longer Arrested!

CHAPTER

SIX

Paul and Silas

The ones around us, who fellowshipped with us (Trish and me), began to call us Paul and Silas (Acts 16). No matter what obstacle came our way, we praised the Lord right on through it, and God empowered us to do so. When opposition would come, our praise and faith grew all the more. Trish would encourage me and let me know that God was still on the throne and had my best interest at heart. She told me that she would be there for me and never leave me nor forsake me, and just as God has kept His promise to me, so has she!

I remember when the enemy found a way to slither in a crack in my door. He tried to infiltrate my spirit and use a woman to get next to me. He took our friendship and added his poison to it. Well, that's what he tried to do! I must admit, he almost succeeded in destroying our friendship. It was cute and cunning. I call the spirit "it" because we wrestle not against flesh and blood, but rulers of darkness in high places (spirits, demonic) (Eph 6:12).

Trish was right there to pray, undergird, understand and hold me up. It did not last long, but too long for me. It seemed like an eternity. The ladies in the choir began to look at me differently and not want me to pray for them. Oh, it hurt, and I was scared of that. The worst part was that I wasn't even attracted to "it". I was still just trying to live right and be her friend because we were in church together and everything. The devil just wanted to tear down what God was building up in that prison. Not being able to pray for God's people was what the enemy knew would hurt me the most.

I fought, and I prayed for that thing to turn me loose. I knew who I was in Christ, and I had to stand my ground. I had never encountered anything like that before. The enemy thought he had me! I didn't fight like he wanted me to fight, but I know my Father in Heaven fought the fight for me! The effective, fervent prayers of the righteous availed much! I was soon Free!! Another chain was broken in my life right in that prison. Today, he (the enemy) could not use that against me because I recognize the signs. Praise the Lord, Hallelujah!!

I thank God for my true best friend. I want the whole world to know that what God has started between she and I, He will perform and complete it.

My hope that if you are reading this book and now this chapter, that you will pray and ask God for someone you can trust to pray with you, and pray you through "anything." That he/she will have your best interest at heart! The word also says to find a friend, show yourself friendly (Prov 18:24). So, I pray you are doing all you can to uplift, encourage and love unconditionally. Especially, someone you call friend!

No Longer Arrested!

CHAPTER SEVEN

Well, it was almost time for me to go home again. I'm excited! November was quickly approaching and I couldn't wait to see my children. It is 2003 and by the time I got home and get settled, it would be 2004.

I was looking forward to getting my life started and returning another parole number. I made up in my mind that I'd get off parole in thirteen months, give back that state number and live for Jesus Christ.

Now, when I touched down in Rialto, Calif., on Nov. 30, 2003, my family was waiting for me at the Ontario Airport. My sons Kaalan and Kaasey were with my parents and all grown up. Kaalan was sixteen years old, and Kaasey was ten years old. My daughter, Kalaon was not with me at the time due to my drug addiction (a whole other story); she was nine years old. They were glad to see me, and I them. Glory to God; I was at home!

I met my parole officer, Steve Day. I was doing well with work and church. I managed to have the same parole officer (p.o.) as my dad; that was a trip! Steve would come by, and we would have coffee and discuss my plans. I really wanted to make it this time.

As time went on, I would relapse again, losing another job and stopped going to church. The hopelessness and despair set in. I began to think, *This is it. I will die like this. What is wrong with me?*

The church I went to at the time had no recovery program, so I sat at my table in our two-bedroom apartment with the yellow pages and called drug programs until I reached the True Vine Women's home in San Bernardino, Calif. It was a 90-180 day program, a Christian program where I would be able to go to church and praise the Lord. That was the best part! However, when I arrived, my spirit told me something different. I hung in there as long as I could because I needed help.

We would go to church at least three times a week and twice on Sunday. We had classes in the mornings, and they were enlightening and helpful, and I was beginning to digest the word. It still seemed like something was missing. I was unfulfilled in that program. The enemy was busy, and I could see it. When the leaders of the church aren't walking upright before God in your face, it's hard to follow them. I knew my life was at stake, but so was my spirit. I decided to leave. Of course, I was talked about and told I was running. I sure was-running for my life! I was called a "Burger King baby" because I wanted things my way. "No, I wanted things right!" Too much was going on that was not Christlike and had nothing to do with recovery. So, I called my parents, and they came to get me.

I stayed clean for a good long while after that. I was still going to church, maintaining my sobriety, and reporting to my parole officer as needed. And I acquired another job. It was with a mortgage company in Riverside, CA. I was blessed with a ride to and from work every day by one of the ladies at church. All was well until that urge came upon me again and instead of calling on the name of Jesus Christ, I fell into the trap of addiction once more!

I was able to buy myself a car in the midst of all of the havoc. I had started renting it out and being stranded. I sold my phone and my soul this time. It wasn't nice! I remember walking the streets of Rialto in a dress and some slippers until I got a ride and went to a man's house I knew. His wife had passed away, and I knew if I went with a little dope and a couple of dollars I'd get in the door. Sure enough he opened the door, and I was welcomed. We got high and when the dope was gone, he asked me to go to bed w/him and when I refused, he got mad and put me out. Now, what was I to do? I thought I had messed up so bad I couldn't go home; I didn't even call or try.

I went outside after trying to reason with him, but he only said, "If you come back with some money, you can stay." Needless to say, I went to Riverside Blvd and began to walk to see if I could find a victim. Not for him because I wasn't anybody's whore and if I do anything for money, it would be for me only. I was the only victim though! I did and of course, I thought it was God answering my prayer. I had already asked if He would put someone in my path to help me. I had nowhere to go.

A truck pulled up and I had my plan together. I would trick him out of his money and have him take me to the dope house, too. It wasn't that easy I found out. I had to really make him believe that I was going to sleep with him before I got a dime. It worked and I came away with enough money to get a lot of dope and alcohol, and I went back to the man's house to change my clothes and use the phone. I gave him a little dope and a beer. I was kind of hungry, but food was the last thing on my mind. I'm just glad I didn't have to sleep with either of them. My plan worked! I had only been away from home a week, but it seemed like five.

I would be gone for even longer though. The guilt and shame of screwing up yet again and leaving my children and what I knew as "home."

While at the guy's house, which I was lodging at, I was introduced to several dealers, and they would be my ticket to stay at his house as long as I needed to. I was paid to cook the powder cocaine into solid rock, and I was paid to transport that cocaine to keep the "man" from getting busted. Who was going to keep me from getting busted? Dummy!! God was keeping me the whole time. I would thank Him as I thought about it. When my adrenaline would race so hard I thought my heart would burst because I was doing things I had no business and getting away with it. Only by the skin of my teeth though. I was the only girl with these guys, and I held as much money, drugs, and guns as they did. I would drive them to various places, and I took a lot of taxicabs also. Just getting the job done!

I would leave the house where I was staying and be dressed as if I were really going somewhere. Off to work I'd go-to the dope house and play bodyguard, watchdog, chauffeur and cook. I was always high though. The drug was so lucrative and in abundance, but it was sickening sometimes.

When the house was raided, I was released and didn't have a place to go. One night I was in the car with some dude and I went to a 7-eleven. I recognized a lady as my cousin, and I called her name Toni Johnson, she turned and screamed my name back. We exchanged words and phone numbers, and I found out that she was in the same business I was in. We hung out together for about three or four days until the idea hit us to go down on Valley Blvd in Rialto and rent a room in the motel by the truck stop (we would be there five months). Psalm 23:4 states, "Yeah, though I walk through the valley of the shadow of death, I will fear no evil."

CHAPTER EIGHT

"How much is it for a room for two nights?" I asked. The manager said, "$120.00." Well, we'll get one night and use the rest to drink and use. Eventually, that would run out so I had to come up with a plan.

We were right next door to the I-10 truck stop, and truckers use too. So, I bought a "sack." I would sell to them to pay for our room, our rock, our drink, our food, and our clothes. Those men were our ticket, and this trip would be longer. Oh yeah, I was also running from the police. I was what was called "absconding." I had not reported to my p.o. since I left home, and every time I saw a cop car, I would freeze, and when they would go by, I'd thaw!

As this kept happening, you'd think I'd go home or go somewhere and clean up my act, but I stayed on the street in the motel, dealing dope and working for the enemy.

I remember having prayer circles right in the midst of my sin and transgressions. The ones who would hang out in my room had to be exposed to Jesus Christ even though I wasn't living right. I knew I wasn't supposed to be in that cesspool, and I needed to go home, so I began to call.

My flesh was definitely warring with my spirit. I'd wake in the mornings and play my gospel music and pray. I know God was keeping me even when I didn't want to be kept! I remember a time when I was about to fight a man because he told me, "How dare you praise the Lord like that. You just took a hit and sold me some dope." I told him, "If you knew like I knew, you'd praise Him, too! He's the reason I'm still able to talk to you after taking this hit and selling you dope!" I exclaimed. He became very rude, and I excused him from my room. He refused to leave, and so I opened one of my knives that I kept at my side (along with a stick and metal pipe at my feet). I opened my door, and he still didn't move. My cousin snatched him out the door, and I tried to cut him after he swung at me. Some of the neighbors upstairs said they would call the police if he didn't leave. I was the one scared, instantly, at that statement, and I ran inside. Come to find out they just said it to get him to leave. Kept again!!

Back inside the room (which was decorated and set up just like an apartment); we had plants, pictures on the walls, pillows and candles. We had a hot plate, crock pot and the microwave and refrigerator was furnished by the motel. We acquired pots, a skillet, plates, glasses (just a couple, mostly plastic) by trading the "rock" for what was needed. That included our clothes, which a booster would bring us also in exchange for rock. So we were pretty well off considering the environment, and if we needed to go, anywhere we caught a taxi. I hardly ever left the room. I had become as close to recluse as I could. I would not even go across the street to the liquor store. I paid someone to run any errands I had. It wasn't because I was totally under the influence all the time either.

No Longer Arrested!

A point had come when I didn't want to be seen outside for fear of being caught by the police. I was safe inside. When the dreaded bamming at the door did come, I was paralyzed! "Open up, police!" That was a familiar sound due to the fact I had been in raids before, but I didn't want to go-yet! My cousin opened the door, but not before I was fully dressed in my starched 501 Levi's, white t-shirt, and white Nikes. If I was going, I was going decent with money in my pocket. I was in the bathroom with my left foot up on the wall and hands in my pockets. The officers showed her some photos of obscounders, and how grateful I was that I wasn't among them.

She laughed at me as I stepped out the bathroom, and immediately, I needed a drink. I sent an order to the store and I was at it again. This was a celebration- I didn't go back to prison; however, I was arrested!!

CHAPTER NINE

The holidays were quickly approaching, and I wanted to see my kids. I called home and to my surprise, my parents brought the boys to visit with me. It was cool! I would soon after get on the city bus and meet them at the movie theater on Baseline and Willow. God was still keeping me!!

Shortly after the holidays, I guess management was tired of our wild parties and running in and out. We were asked to leave. We didn't at first. It took a couple of days, and we even would sneak in and out, and I would pay for another room in someone else's name, and I'd pay them to do it. That meant we had to stay in that particular room without coming out, so not to be seen by management or any haters. It really didn't matter because we had all we thought was needed from food to liquor, clothes, porno movies, and music.

Eventually, we left and I would wind up in the north part of San Bernardino in Motel 6. My cousin and I were separated, and I wouldn't see her again for a long time. I began selling dope up there and duping guys out of their money and cars. Again, I had it going on, so I thought. To be very honest, this lifestyle was tiring and arduous. I remember praying and asking God to see me through another trial. I wanted out but didn't want to go back to prison. I wanted the easy way out of course. I managed to gravitate toward everything that was negative, and it seemed like that was how it was going to stay. I knew I'd never be free because I was in bondage within my soul, within my mind. I was yoked up and entangled with witchcraft, deceit, cheating, perversion, and lying just to name a few unlikely spirits. Let me not sugar-coat this-demonic spirits!! They had attached themselves to me, and I welcomed them, even deep within somewhere I knew there was something different about me.

Whenever I'd run to the church house, I felt right at home, but I couldn't seem to stay long enough to get what God had for me. When I'd run to the dope house, I felt like a fish out of water. Somehow the enemy made me welcomed, and everybody liked me and made the drugs easy to get, and the victims came easier, too.

God forgive me!? I'd find myself asking that over and over again. I was wrong for doing what I was doing, but I had to survive!

The next day, Hope and I were getting dressed and planning another rendezvous with the devil. I was already showered and together, as I was listening to Mariah Carey and finishing my packing. She went in the bathroom to get ready and all of a sudden, a loud pound at the door. Oh, no! Not again! I exclaimed. Yep, again! "Open up. It's the police; Come on I see you in there," he said. The curtain was pulled back ever so slightly, but I could see him, and he could see me sitting on the bed. "Damn!" I said loudly. I almost got away.

They came in, and Hope wasn't dressed from the waist down, so after they apprehended her, I was told to put her pants on and her shoes. They asked the necessary questions and all the time I was running, I had my alias ready, but when he asked me who I was I told him the truth. While putting the cuffs on her and reading her rights, they told me to leave. With my purse and CD player in tow, I left the room and thought I was "scott- free." I went upstairs on the third floor; they took her to the police car. Within minutes a knock came at the door; it was them coming for me! I was arrested again. Off to the city jail I went!

While there, I called home and informed my family what had transpired. My mom was relieved that I was arrested at least she knew where I was.

Within a couple of hours, I was at West Valley Detention Center for another walk through. I knew I would go straight to prison. I was glad I didn't have additional charges to my absconding. I began to pray and ask God to have mercy on me and allow me to be continued on parole (cop'd). I wanted to do right. I was worn out, and this was my way to rest and do right.

I was shipped to C.I.W (California Institution for Women), in Norco, CA, where I'd spend twenty-one days. I was c.o.p.'d, and I was home in time for Kaalan's graduation from high school.

No Longer Arrested!

CHAPTER TEN

My parents and kids moved to Victorville in 2005. Kaalan was enrolled in Silverado High School and Kaasey in Mesa Linda Middle School. The graduation was June 16, 2005, and I was in the brink. I needed to be at Kaalan's graduation!

While in C.I.W., I prayed in my two-man cell, on the yard, and went to church services as much as I could. I would be in reception for a while, so we only went out every other day (just like in Chowchilla). Prayerfully, church fell on my day out and a shower. After two weeks, the women began to realize I was serious about Christ, and they began to ask me to pray at night before bed. So, I'd stand at the little tiny window in the door and pray where they could hear me down the corridor. I could hear them saying "Yes, Lord; Please, Lord; and Thank you, Lord." I was blessed beyond measure. When I said, "Amen, in the Name of Jesus Christ, Amen", they would yell "Amen," and it would echo through the cemented hall way. In the morning when we'd come out for chow, the women would be expressing how well they slept and how much better the felt. Bless the Lord; Bless His Name in the Highest!!

I was trying to be as jovial and encouraging as I could. To see the movement of God in the C.I.W., not only in the women, but the officers as well was amazing. They were few and far between, however, they'd let you know in so many little ways that they cared. As I would fix it in my mind to focus on the moment or the day at hand, it made my life there more content. (No matter what state I am I learned to be abased, or abound...Phil 4:11-13). I was able to be of service and enjoy it. Oh, I wished everyday that my parole officer, Steve Day, would show his face and release me, but I was blessed. God had me, and I knew it!

It was a Friday afternoon, and we had the day to stay inside (rotation). I was up on my bunk, reading and looking out the window when I heard the door click and then a man called loudly, "Williams, W98282," then again, "Williams, W98282!" I jumped down (heart beating fast) and answered, "Yes, here I am." "Step out," he said, "Your P.O. is here. Go in the kitchen." My insides began to shake and quake, and all I could say was, "Thank you, thank you, Lord!" Not knowing the outcome, but having more faith than a mustard seed, I sat across from him. He looked larger than life (he was well over six feet anyway) sitting there with my file opened in front of him.

"Hi, Steve," I said, still shaking. He peered up from the file and said, "What's up? So, you finally got caught, huh? What do you have to say for yourself?" I began to tear up, and I shared with him that I was afraid to come in and see him when I first relapsed because I didn't want to come back to places like these, but here I am anyway. He explained to me the terms of being continued on parole and said that I qualified. He proceeded with saying that he knew I was a good lady and I am capable of much better. Because he has been to my home and observed how my parents and I get along and I have some good home training and strong belief system, he was going to let me go. I was so elated and relieved! I would see Kaalan graduate. The only thing was, it was a Friday and no releases over the weekend. I would wait until Monday morning. I asked him before he left if he would call my folks, tell them, and give them directions. He said he would be glad to and wished me good luck!!

Over the weekend, I sang louder and prayed harder and cried more because I wanted to make sure I left everything God gave me for those women I would leave behind. My cellie, China, was a young lady who was facing a few years, and we bonded while I was there those twenty-one days. She gave me her father's phone number and asked me to call him and tell him she loved him. It was my pleasure to do so.

Well, Monday morning was upon me, and it seemed like forever for them to call my name. I waited, supposedly patiently, but when they came for me I almost started running. The sergeant took my DNA swab. That was in case I committed another crime, and I'd be in the system. She took my fingerprints again and ran my nationwide (alias included). I came up clean, so they had to surely let me go!

I would be released in that ugly moomoo (I spoke of it in the beginning), and when I stepped outside, my mom and dad were waiting for me to take me home! Hallelujah! They laughed at me all the way in that moomoo!

We finally made it to Victorville. I was home-again!!! The prodigal daughter had returned home and the Father welcomed her home (Luke 15:22-24).

CHAPTER ELEVEN

It was June, 2005, and I would see Kaalan graduate! What a blessing! He was glad I was home, and so was I. The ceremony was held at the Glen Helen Amphitheater, and it was very nice. I was so proud of Kaalan and all his friends who had made it!

My mom had been diagnosed with kidney failure, and it was not going to be easy for her. So, I became her caregiver and would help with her dialysis and meds. I thought this would keep me home and clean and sober. It did for awhile!

I joined Burning Bush Baptist Church and began going to service regularly and bible study. I enjoyed going there. I joined the usher board and sang in the choir, too. Pastor Denson made room for me to share my testimony with the congregation on one Sunday morning. It had an impact on a few women, and they had opened up to me and were glad I had stepped up and shared. I was free and doors began to open for me. I had a job, access to my parents' cars and was paying my bills. I was asked to read poems at our women's conferences, and I was having a ball!

I met two very good friends whom I love and care about to this day - Gerolyn Howard and Tasha Phillips. We started a ministry of going to the park downtown Victorville where the homeless would reside and go with hopes of a meal or two.

We made hygiene bags and took clothes, shoes, and Our Lord and Savior Jesus Christ with us on the fourth of every month. There would be other churches there, and they would have hot food. We would take pictures and our children would help with them. At the end, we would have a huge prayer circle, hug and talk with them and fellowship together. I was blessed at the opportunity to give back to God's people, to share with them what He had done for me.

It was a sad day when the City of Victorville stopped us from coming down there, and eventually, the park was made into a parking lot. No more trees, grass, playground, kids or feeding of the homeless. How sad!

I would stay at the Bush for a couple of years, and in that time, I would join the intercessory prayer team and start my prison ministry. I was faithful, and God was moving. I was right where I was supposed to be, so I thought!

I started to feel like a fish out of water. I knew I was full, and my spirit was leaping inside me with word. I knew I was supposed to be doing more, and I wanted to talk to my pastor, so I did! I wrote him a letter and went to his office. We talked after I read the letter expressing my call and desire to spread/speak the word of God, to do as I know that God had told me. But I would still sit!

I relapsed, and when I left home, I went to San Bernardino and found my cousin. I would stay with her a while, and this time it seemed way too comfortable, like I belonged there, so I stayed. There was so much going on inside me - warring. My good and bad, my right and my wrong, my light and my dark, my flesh and my spirit!

Everything that was not of God was winning. No matter how many gospel songs I listened to or how many prayers I prayed, it felt as though it was getting nowhere. God wasn't listening to me anymore. That's what I had convinced myself of, and it made my drug abuse less work. I tried to make it fun and stayed drunk so I couldn't feel or think about what I was falling into - bondage of arrest!!

The holidays were coming around, and I called home, and I was welcomed. I came home broken and blistered, down and depressed. I wouldn't even look at myself in the mirror; every time I did, I cried. I couldn't stand myself.

I would go back to the Bush and try to fit in again! I found myself in recovery at St. John of God, in Victorville. At first, I thought, *This is not going to work because I am supposed to be high and drunk. I'm supposed to be down and out. No matter what, this won't work!*

Time went by, and I began to be involved. From the first seven days I spent in detox, to the end, I blossomed and shared, and I loved recovery! This was not like any other time. I got myself a sponsor, participated in group, and I noticed a big change.

The men and women there were concerned about each other's recovery and life was good. I made friends and even fell in love. Wow! But most of all, I liked who I saw in the mirror. I was even voted vice president of the facility. I would learn how to cope with my feelings, my guilt of giving my daughter up at birth. I'd received a letter from CPS earlier that year, and they informed me that they had my daughter, and I had a chance of getting her back.

In my addiction, I gave up my baby, Kalaon. I had just had Kaasey and wasn't strong enough or clean enough to take care of her. I also thought I lost her forever, but God yet again gave me another chance. So, while in St. John's, I became stronger and when it was time for me to graduate, I knew I was free from bondage, and I left everything there that wasn't good for me! I stayed clean a year and went back to St. John's as the supervisor in the kitchen. I really felt like I was a part of life. I was living! I was growing! God is good!!

CHAPTER TWELVE

I relapsed again! I was at work one day and found myself in San Bernardino with a pipe in my mouth and the dealer on my phone. It was the fall of 2007, and I had lost my job all because I didn't call in! I was high, I was drunk, I was guilty and ashamed. There was no way this time I was going back. I let down all the women I had gotten a connection with at St. John's. How was I to ever go back and show my face? Bro. Gary (the director) had given me a chance, above all those other applicants with much more experience and clean time than me. I couldn't go back! I had let my family down again. My mom being sickly and the promises I had made to my kids. How was I to go back? I let myself down, and once more, I let God down!

I remember going to True Light Christian Fellowship with my kids, and I knew I could call Pastor Rosalind, but I didn't. I could call her when I couldn't call my own mother or my pastor. Don't misunderstand me, my mom was there for me always, but it was altogether different. I kept saying I was going to call, but I didn't. I knew I couldn't call my current church because I was already told that if I messed up again they were done with me!

I stayed gone all the way until just before Christmas. I would somehow get up enough courage to call home, and I'd make it in time for Christmas. My family welcomed me home, but it was rough!

At the beginning of 2008, I went to visit True Light (the third Sunday in Jan.). My parents and I went, and we sat in the back of the church. Service was well under way, when the spirit of the living God told me to join church. I sent a note to the pulpit, and Pastor Charles read it and gave it to Pastor Rosalind. She stopped the service and had me come to the front, and I cried like a baby. I never felt so free and loved at a church. I was home!

Pastor Rosalind came down from the pulpit to embrace me and Prophetess Gamble prayed over me. I knew there had been a change in me at that moment!

I would begin to be active, and the next thing I knew, I was in the second row from the front, with Sis. Regina. Pastor Rosalind had always told me that I was meant to be at True Light, and she knew in her spirit that's why she prayed me in. She and Pastor Charles had allowed me to be a part of the service, and I was reading my poems and brought into leadership. I was clean and sober for seven months, and God blessed me with a car, and He birthed my prison ministry "The Power in the Pen-n- Prison" at True Light. I took the Vision and Mission Statement to the pastors. They blessed it, and it is still in existence today. I was working as a caregiver for a nice lady Ms. Mary and I was going to work every day and enjoying it. When I first started the job, I was catching the bus; I had come a long way!

No Longer Arrested!

On June 29, 2008, I had been blessed with the opportunity to bring the word before the congregation. I was excited! Pastor had already shared with me that she and the Apostle decided to have me go forth to prepare for my evangelist license. At first, I couldn't believe it. Me? This addict and ex-con. I knew I had dreamed of one day being licensed and being able to share my testimony with those who were arrested, and God would free them by the seed planted.

It was happening so quickly, and I would prepare my message and a praise dance as well. That Sunday morning on my 42nd birthday, I stood before God's people and my message was titled "There's a Storm Brewing, Hallelujah, It's Raining!" (Leviticus 26).

After service that day, we went to eat at Red Robin for my birthday, and Pastor Rosalind told me to be ready for the Holy Convocation. I would be licensed! Glory to God! Glory to God! He kept His promise to me; now I had to keep mine! How blessed I am!

CHAPTER THIRTEEN

Doing what I said I'd never do again...I went to San Bernardino. My boyfriend had gotten out of prison, and rushing to go see him, I thought I could do it and make it back home unscathed. I found myself not only fighting with him, but others! I was selling dope again, so I had to carry a knife. Now mind you, I'm a licensed evangelist now-it's 2009. I also started running in some of the circles that I didn't want to, but needed to, in order to survive down there! I even made plans to transport drugs again and go to Vegas and make money. The word tells us that when the evil man comes back to the house and finds it swept and empty, he then takes seven other spirits with him (Matthew 12:43-45).

Losing my car to violence and run-ins from the police wasn't enough. I stayed down there and continued selling dope, smoking and drinking, lying, and doing whatever. Now, when I say whatever, I'm not talking about, as far as, whatever in a sexual nature. I'm talking about what I needed to do selling, cheating, scheming etc. to keep my party going. Some party...because I wasn't having any fun!

My boyfriend began to sleep with someone I thought was my friend, which led me to fighting with her. Some days, I thought I had to fight both of them. However, the biggest fight I had was within me. The war that was raging on the inside of me was uncontrolled, and as a result, it wound up being at least another week before I would come home!

It was the guilt, shame and self-pity that kept me, and I thought if I could get high enough I wouldn't feel anything! The hopelessness had saturated me. I had succumbed to despair, and I just knew "this is it if I don't get out!"

God, my Heavenly Father answered yet another prayer. Because the enemy was upon me as a flood, God raised up a standard for me. He opened the lines of communication for me to come home, and soon thereafter, my parents came for me! I thought, Thank you Jesus Christ, for an escape and my parents (1 Cor. 10:13).

I didn't go right back to church, but everyone knew I was home! I was glad to be home. More glad than I ever had been before! I had a lapse in judgment that I thought was going to kill me dead in sin. Oh, God, my Heavenly Father, my keeper, I thank You for new mercies. I thank You for another chance to get this thing right!

I made it to church, Hallelujah! I was still a little shaky, but I knew I was safe. I knew at True Light, I was safe and I'd be ok. I was ready to be loved, and I didn't want to see the "boogie man" anymore! I had left him in the streets, and I was free!

CHAPTER FOURTEEN

Suddenly, Pastor Rosalind took me and loved on me. She allowed the spirit of the Lord to bring me right back to where I had left, and she moved as God told her, concerning me.

I was asked to do the congregational prayer three Sundays in a row and she kept me close to her. My spirit was ready, my heart was ready and willing, but my mind was telling me "You won't make it; you're going to fail again." However, I kept on moving, I kept on praising, I kept on believing, I kept on claiming my deliverance, my healing, my restoration, my breakthrough! I kept on trusting the Lord and my pastors!

I had to trust the Lord because at one point, I almost forgot who I was, who I am in Christ Jesus! That I am the righteousness of Christ Jesus (2Cor. 5:21); I am strong in the Lord and the Power of His might (Eph.6:10); I am more than a conqueror (Rom. 8:37); I am not moved by what I see (2Cor.4:18); I am walking by faith, not by sight (2Cor. 5:7); I am daily overcoming the devil(1John 4:4); I am an overcomer by the blood of the Lamb and the word of my testimony (Rev. 12:11); I am learning to present my body as a living sacrifice, holy and acceptable unto God, which is my reasonable service (Rom. 12:1); and I am truly delivered from the powers of darkness (Col 1:13).

I AM NO LONGER ARRESTED!!!!!!

It's a year later, and I am more convinced than ever that I am a child of God (Rom. 8:16), and I am free from all manner of evil, perversion and hindrance! I walk in the Power and Authority of who I am in Christ Jesus!

My pastor has followed in the obedience of God and has me as her armor bearer (I'm still in awe sometimes). God allowed me to continue in the ministry He gave me two years ago. The Power-in-the-Pen-n Prison Ministry where I write into prisons sharing my experience, strength and hope with men and women. I am finished with my first book! My relationship with my kids has blossomed, and my mom and I are closer than ever! More on my relationships in Volume II. I am an aspiring baker with a dream to also have my own business someday- Kellee's Kakes and Kookies.

Since I have surrendered and let go and let God, I haven't stopped. God has taken me to higher heights and deeper depths and I'm truly excited about my new life today!

I pray that something was said or done in my testimony to change, encourage, and/or convince someone that they too can live "NO LONGER ARRESTED."

I remember sitting in a cell wondering when I'd be free.
I remember sitting, wondering if God remembered me.
When I was arrested, my physical body was locked up and my Spirit was too!
I seemed to have this weight upon me and didn't know what to do.

But one day, I called upon the greatest name I know and at that moment my cell began to glow.

I knew then I'd be free and God had not forgotten me.

The enemy tried to tell me that I'd always be bound; he's a lie.

Because of Christ, a new life I've found!

Being arrested doesn't mean always behind bars and walls,

I know today, I'm no longer arrested at all!!

ABOUT THE AUTHOR

Born and raised in Altadena, Ca. in 1966, in a middle class neighborhood, Kellee Williams was with her parents, and she was baptized in and an active member of Lincoln Avenue Baptist Church, in Pasadena at a very early age. She loved going to church, bible study, vacation bible school, youth camp at Thousand Pines and winning oratorical contests. She graduated from John Muir High School with honors and was active in sports. But, she never thought her life would take the turns that it did!

Unexpectedly and suddenly, Kellee went from attending college at the University of Arkansas at Little Rock to selling dope and in a gang and eventually smoking cocaine and trafficking to different states. She went from getting an education in journalism to the school of hard knocks and streets of insanity!

It has taken over twenty years of drug abuse, prison terms, rapes, physical abuse, etc to get her to this point! God has parted her Red Sea and brought her over to His side on dry land, and she knows for a fact He gets all the praise for breaking shackles, destroying yokes and setting her FREE!

Today, she is a licensed evangelist and is the visionary/founder of The Power-in-the-Pen-n Prison Ministry (8 years). She is looking to have her own business/building one day for "Kellee's Kakes and Kookies." She is a team leader in the Kairos Prison ministry, and she is a member of a powerful prayer group called "The Watchmen who don't Come Down."

Evangelist Kellee Williams is a member of Abundant Living Family Church, in the High Desert where Mark and Kendra Graham are the awesome, devoted pastors! She loves life today. Even on her worst day, being sober and clean is much greater than her best day being high and dysfunctional. Praise the Most High God!

www.ingramcontent.com/pod-product-compliance
Lightning Source LLC
Chambersburg PA
CBHW071201090426
42736CB00012B/2411